Funny Si
volume 3

Dalesman

First published in 2020 by Dalesman Publishing
an imprint of
Country Publications Ltd
The Gatehouse, Skipton Castle
Skipton, North Yorkshire BD23 1AL

ISBN 978-1-85568-388-4

Printed in China by 1010 Printing International Ltd.

Introduction

The world is full of signs — telling us what to do, and when, or what not to do, and why not. Luckily, though, not all are serious and there are plenty that provoke a wry smile, whether deliberately or not.

Here we've collected some of the funniest signs and notices contributed by readers of the *The Dalesman* and *The Countryman* magazines. Many thanks to all those readers who have submitted signs over the years — we hope they raise a chuckle!

Mill Yard Parking
MONDAY - FRIDAY BETWEEN 8AM - 5PM
THIS CAR PARK IS FOR PATRONS OF MILL YARD BUSINESSES ONLY
Maximum 2 Hours Stay
PATRONS STAYING OVER 2 HOURS, PLEASE GET A FROG PARKING
STICKER FROM THE BUSINESS YOU ARE VISITING
Frog parking
ONLY
All others will be 'Toad'

Disable Toilet

20
MPH
Please
drive carefully
through the
village

CAUTION
Mouth
Watering
Hot Cross
Buns...
Floor May
Be Slippery!
Bakers Delight

COLD DRINKS
99
Flake
OFTEN LICKED BUT NEVER BEATEN
CONES

NO SMOKING
EXCEPT GUIDE DOGS
buy your
stamps

Ivyhouse Cottages
The Rest of
The World

Dr Bell
Surgeon Extraordinaire
Limbs amputated
Teeth pulled
Boils lanced

WC
URINALS
24 HR FACILITIES AVAILABLE
AT STATION CAR PARK
TWO HOUR
MAXIMUM STAY
A FREE TICKET MUST BE DISPLAYED
Restrictions
Apply 7 Days a Week

Janet BAAH
John LAMB
THURSDAY
MAY 2ND

cafe opening times:
open most days about 12:00
occasionly as early as 09:00
some days as late as 15:00
we close about 19:00 or
midnight, occasionally at
23:00, but sometimes as late
as 04:00. Somedays we are
not here at all, but lately
we are here most of the time,
exept when we are somewhere
else. Ian & Patricia.

barber shop:

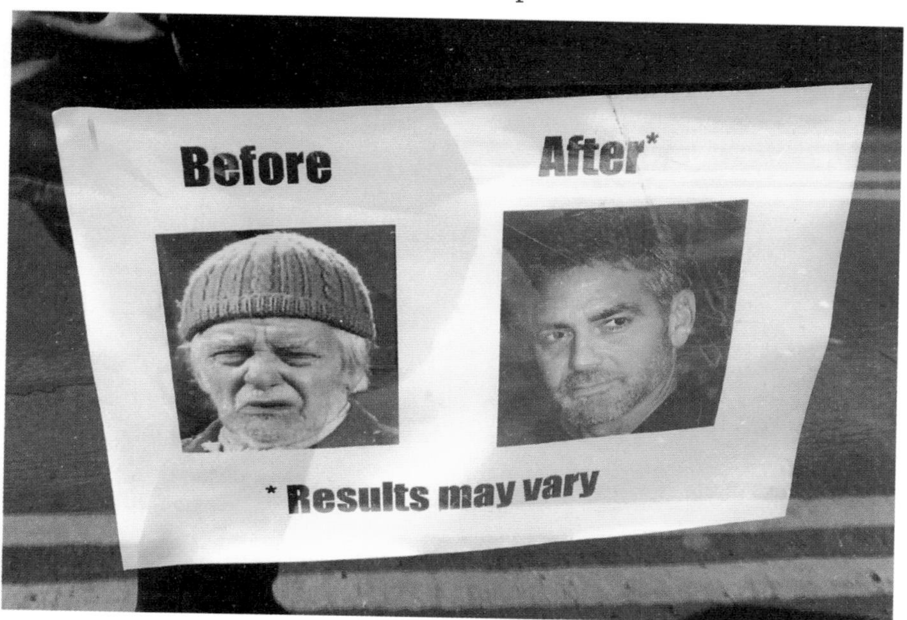

Ben Nevis Inn
WEATHER FORECASTING STONE
CONDITION
FORECAST
Stone is Wet
Rain
Stone is Dry
Not Raining
Shadow on Ground
Sunny
White on Top
Snowing
Can't see Stone
Foggy
Swinging Stone
Windy
Stone Jumping Up & Down
Earthquake
Stone Gone
Tornado

DO NOT
CROSS THIS FIELD
Unless you can do it
in 9 seconds
Because the
BULL can do it in 10

Please note:
The post-apocalyptical
fiction section
has been moved to
Current Affairs.
ROBERT LENKIEW
ALICE
FOWEY ALBUM

CAUTION
SLOW MOVING
BRUSH IN ROAD

CATS EYES
REMOVED

This bench is dedicated to
the men who lost the will
to live whilst following their
partners around the shoe shops
of Chester.

CHICKENS -
PLEASE CLOSE
THE GATE

WATER
FOR YOUR
DOG
...OR REALLY
SHORT PEOPLE
WITH LOW
STANDARDS ..
.. WE DON'T
JUDGE

WOLVERHAMPTON COUNCIL
COMMUNITY
RECYCLING
CENTRE
Any queries or suggestions

PLEASE DO NOT ALLOW YOUR DOG TO FOWL ON THE FOOTPATH.

ETHEL ROAD
THE UNREADY

GLUE HILL
PLEASE STICK TO
THE PAVEMENT

Guard Dog
on duty
3 days a Week ....
you guess
Which days !!

LIGHTHOUSE ROAD
NO ACCESS TO LIGHTHOUSE

DELI
CORNISH
GIN
SANDWICHES

THE
CHARLTON ARMS
HUSBAND
DAY CARE CENTRE
- NEED TIME TO YOURSELF?
- NEED TIME TO RELAX?
- WANT TO GO SHOPPING?
LEAVE YOUR HUSBAND HERE
WE LOOK AFTER HIM FOR YOU
YOU ONLY PAY FOR HIS DRINK'S!
01584 872813

TRUST
Market leader in replacement parts
and accessories for all makes of tractor
Vapormatic is a brand you can trust
DAVID BROWN
MUD 264

PRIVATE
NO ENTRY
NO LANDING
NO FISHING
NO LIGHTING FIRES
NO RAPPING OR HOOTING

Parish Church
Service road

Courtown Tidy Towns
DANGER
Electrified Grass
Activated
by Dog
Poop

Party*
functions
CATERED FOR...
Weddings & Separations
Promotions & Demotions
Celebrations & Condolences
Break ups & Make ups
Leavings & Grievings

SOMERSET & DORSET RAILWAY

COMPANY RULE

Enginemen are Forbidden to blow their whistles or Drain Cocks whilst standing in the station. as this may frighten horses and alarm passengers. Furthermore. Leaking Cocks must be attended to. A fine of sixpence for each Leaking Cock will be strictly enforced

1864

By Order

PLEASE HANG ON
YOUR REAR VIEW MIRROR NOW AND
FOR THE DURATION OF VOYAGE

SLOW DOWD
CHILDREN AND
OAPS PLAYING
IN THE ROAD

Please
don't flush

Nappies, sanitary towels,
paper towels, gum,
old phones, unpaid bills,
junk mail, your ex's sweater,
hopes, dreams or goldfish

Down this
toilet

Toilets
Unsuitable
for motors

Unsupervised kids
will be given free
espressos and
puppies!!!

SECRET BUNKER

CATTLE
Close these
gates at night
and at all times
QMS 10054

South Shropshire
District Council
PUBLIC TOILETS
InterPublic
Have you
Paid and Displayed

EQUINE
EXCRETA
GRATIS.
PLEASE
RETURN

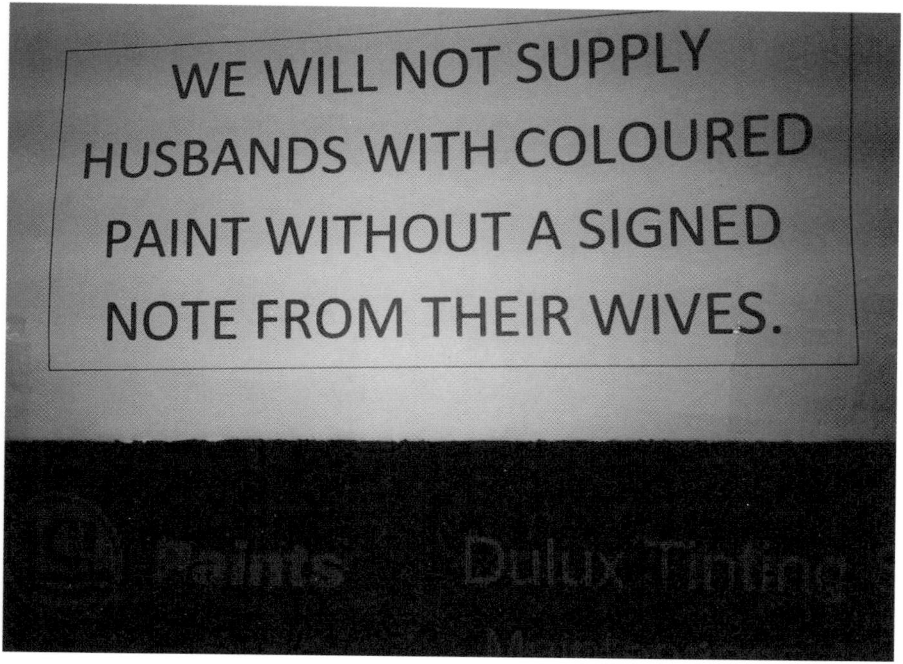

WE WILL NOT SUPPLY
HUSBANDS WITH COLOURED
PAINT WITHOUT A SIGNED
NOTE FROM THEIR WIVES.

WEEDS
FOR SALE
-PICK YOUR OWN

TEMPRIE SYNE
WORTHEN

GREENCOMBE
GARDENS
OPEN 2-6
April May June & July
HEAVY
PLANT
CROSSING

VICTORIAN
I·PAD
£2·95

CAUTION

VEHICLES MUST NOT
ENTER THIS SHED WHEN
DOORS ARE CLOSED

BY ORDER

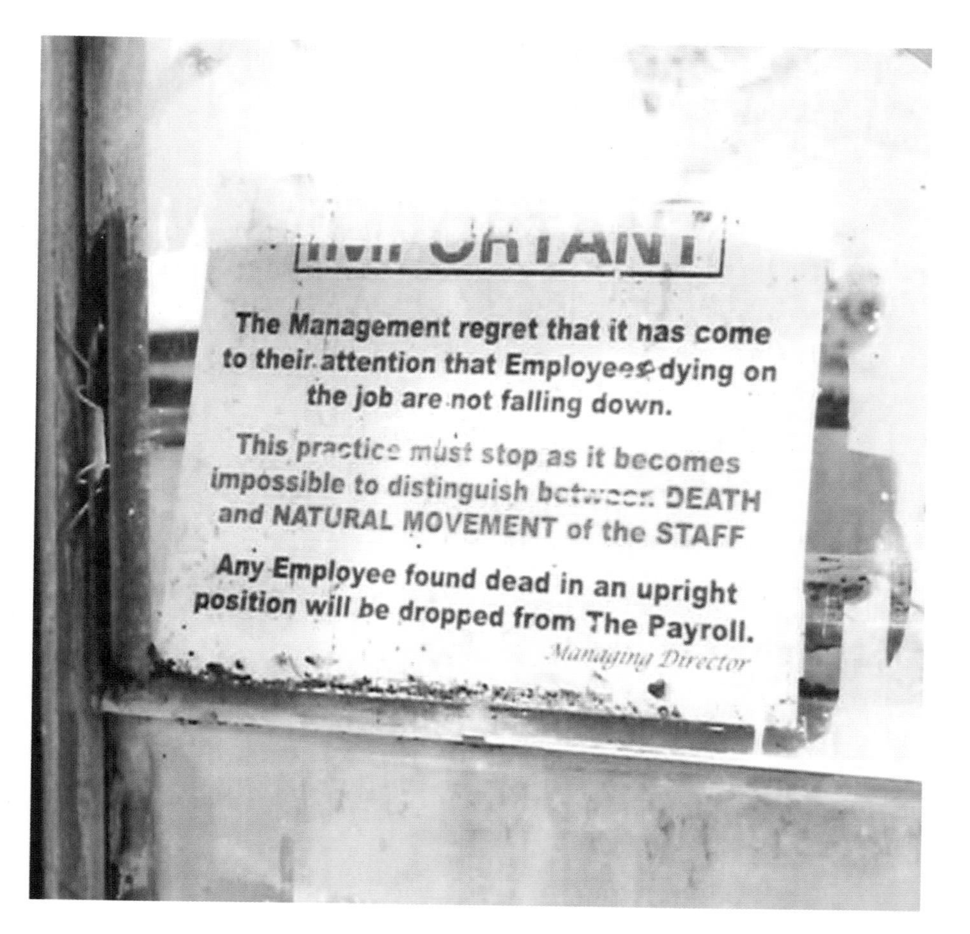
The Management regret that it has come
to their attention that Employees dying on
the job are not falling down.
This practice must stop as it becomes
impossible to distinguish between DEATH
and NATURAL MOVEMENT of the STAFF
Any Employee found dead in an upright
position will be dropped from The Payroll.
Managing Director

Please close
the gate

FIRE ALARM
WHEN THIS
SOUNDS PLEASE CALL
FIRE BRIGADE

IS THERE LIFE
AFTER DEATH?
TRESPASS
HERE AND
FIND OUT!

YOU ARE WELCOME TO BRING
YOUR DOG INSIDE
CHILDREN HOWEVER MUST
BE KEPT ON A LEAD

Compost Drive Thru
Now Open

Northbound
Southbound

SLOW
LAMBS
CHASE
CARS

SLOW
SHEEP
CROSSING

HAM ½
SANDWICH 3

ERECTED TO THE MEMORY OF
CAPT R. C. B. PARTRIDGE M.C., Cde G.
KILLED IN ACTION SEPT 28. 1918
BY FRIENDS IN SOUTH WALES.

PIDLEY SHEEP
LANE

HORSE +
PONY
TRACKING

HORSES
Unicorns

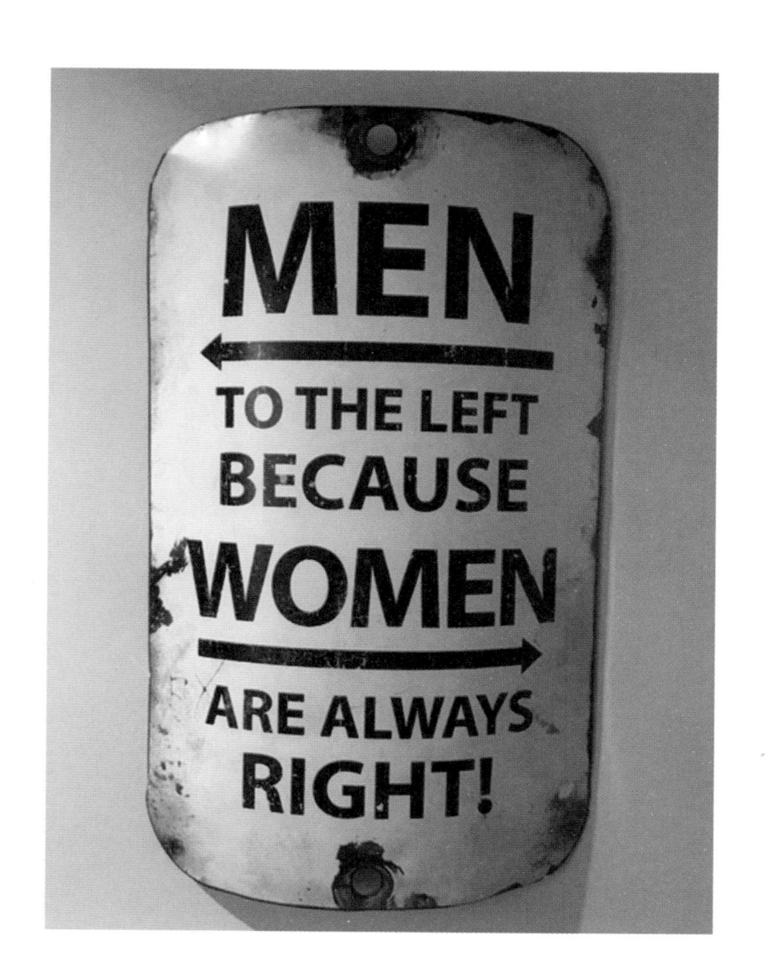
MEN
TO THE LEFT
BECAUSE
WOMEN
ARE ALWAYS
RIGHT!

Want to start FREE Yoga?
Please Start by bending over
and picking up your dog poo!
(Known as the "Downward Dog Position")
THEN POOP IT IN THE BIN!
THANKYOU ROB BRADDICK.
#yogapoo #visitwestwardho
BRADDICKS
LEISURE

Canal &
River Trust
Caution:
Ducks at play
Please be sensitive: don't mention
plum sauce or l'orange.
Charity no. 1146792
Enjoy, volunteer, donate | canalrivertrust.org.uk

SWINTON PARK
TREKKING CENTRE
BIRDS OF PREY
COOKERY SCHOOL

PUBLIC BRIDAL
WAY
STOPS METRE
AHEAD

BUY ONE BEER
FOR THE PRICE
OF TWO
AND RECEIVE
THE SECOND BEER
absolutley
FREE!

FREE
HORSE
MANURE
FILL YOUR
BOOTS

Barbon Village Hall
CHILDRENS PLAYING FIELD
NO DOGS
IF YOUR CHILDREN ARE PLAYING
ON THE EQUIPMENT OR ON THE GRASS
& YOU HAVE A DOG OR DOGS
PLEASE TIE THEM TO THE POST

NO
ROAD
MARKINGS

SPACE TOILET
CONTACT
KEARNS PROPERTIES:
01943 605960
KEARNS
PROPERTIES
DIRECT
ENQUIRIES:
01377 249109

Home
cooked
fresh
local

PUB CRAFT
YORK'S
BEST
AIR CONDITIONING
BRIGANTES

Acknowledgements

Thanks to the following for submitting photographs:

Jane Adolph
Jenny Allen
Rachel Allen
Roger Allen
Mary Ball
R Barnes
Astrid Bartlett
Michael Bass
Brian Blundell
Christine Bradley
Martin Broadribb
Phil Calvert
Clive & Chris Carroll
Andy Chapman
Wendy Charman
Phil Clarke
Andy Coates
Mr Cooper
Jean Creasey
Barry Davis
Anthony Davison
Esther De Groot
Devon County Show
Janet Dolby
M J Dorling
Liz Downes
Thomas Edgar
Robin Field
Lisa Firth
Clemency Fox
Linda Frost
Ron Gordon
John Gulliver
Olivia Haslett
Stephanie Hilborne
Kim Horstmanshof
Tony Howard
John Husband
Paul & Jackie Inness
Rev David Johnson
Tracey Johnson
Margaret Kilner
John McCaig
Edward Mcnaghten
James Miller
Anthony Pearce
Alan Prescott
Willie Shand
Colin Silvester
Amrit Singh
Charles Spottiswoode
Simone Stanbrook-Byrne
Jack Stone
Jim Stronach
John Timbrell
Bob Walker
John White
Mrs S White
Mark Whitley
David Williams
Pauline Williams
Ian Willson
Chas Woodhouse